Belly-up Rosehip:

a Tongue Blue with Mud Songs

Swimming with Elephants
PUBLICATIONS

ISBN-13: 978-1-950375-05-9
(Swimming with Elephants Publications)

Belly-up Rosehip:

a Tongue Blue with Mud Songs

Tyler Dettloff

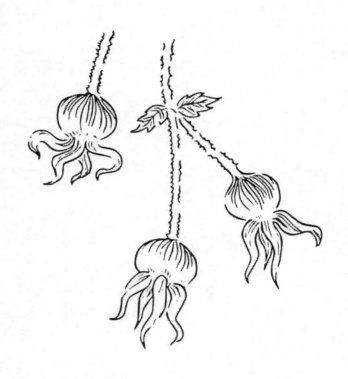

Contents

Thunder Burnt (A Northern Blues Prayer)..............1

Section 1: Spit

I Reach Through Flies 5

To Keep Away Crows Feet 6

Licking Lures 8

Salt Peanuts 10

Cranes Too Early, Trout Too Late...................... 11

Gnaw and Tame 13

Mètis Breakfast...14

Finger Painted and Blood Drawn 15

Surefooted Spring-fed Salt Lick 16

Section 2: Shout

Daffodil Yawp...21

Dynamite Honey 22

With Bloody Fangs Just Like Yours (*Wiindigo Mishkwiiwidoone*)......................................23

Southpaw Gnome 26

Swamp Sap 29

Mouthwash 30

Section 3: Eat

Cranberry Four-Ten 32

Spuds Are Heavy 36

The Doors Left Unlocked 39

Juncos and Buntings 40

What the Soil Forgot 42

Quill Remembers the Oxbow 44

Caution like Fiver 46

Section 4: Tell

Cleaning Trout 48

Honey High and Nectar Prone 51

She's Got Sugar 53

Churn...54

Hemlock Ain't For Hillbillies 55

Tomato Juice 56

You Must Be a Murder...57

Thousands of Frogs Croaking Purple...................59

Nibi Bimaadezewin (A Prayer for Travel) 61

For Minokami

Thunder Burnt (A Northern Blues Prayer)

O baby please,
tell me you won't let me change my ways.
O baby please,
tell me you want me all my days

in the thunder burnt sweet grass,
the red-root cinnamon.
Behind the purple house there's a spectacle—
ghost rice dances *minomiin.*
And I swallow my tongue.
And I swallow my tongue.
And I swallow my tongue.
And I swallow my

O baby please,
tell me you'll leave amphetamines.
O baby please,
hear me *Baawating Gnoozhekaaning.*

O baby please,
tell me to change my ways.
O baby please,
hear me that I want you all my days

and I'll unbraid
my *animikii* tied tongue.

Section 1: Spit

"Strings of spit testify to the bark I've kissed."

- Cecily Parks, *O'Nights*

I Reach Through Flies

to weavings in the grass.

Could be a defunct sparrow nest
beaten by thunder and rain
nitrate blades sanitized in sand
that beg birds for a second weave.

Or it could be dog shit
ripened in sunshine
once a coiled defecation of relief
that begs dogs for a second taste.

O, the leaves of grass
always stink this close
to the solstice.

To Keep Away Crows Feet

I watched a dozen red wing black birds
fight over a single maggot in the church parking lot
as funeral barkers repeated the priest.
The birds smeared that crawler into a grease
to bake on the blacktop. Maggot resin
waxed their beaks. Soon I will gather
fiddlehead ferns, place their fuzz
on my tongue. I thought about paving
my driveway, left it dirt instead.
I won't reseed the lawn either.
I can smell the bog's breath.
Thickets are not fallow.

Last winter I crept to the crawlspace
slept away four moons. When I awoke
I could only stomach tubers and a few berries.
But I wanted meat in my mouth.

Mayflies hatch and we tie bait
to match. Fingertips gaunt and sharp
from feathers and thread, a tight quilt
knit to moisten trout tongues.
Fly rod flits cast spells over swamp streams.
I do not understand trout rising in the thaw
but I damn sure know comfort
in the underbelly of a bog.
Worms and maggots pump their little hearts
all winter long between roots and decay.
I plug my ears with mourning dove songs.

If we traveled like birds
we'd grow fat and pretty.
My hands would soften.
I'd moisturize my crows feet and fallow heart.
At every funeral I'd say the same thing.
I'd knead spruce sap against my gums
and ask the needles to have mercy on my tongue.

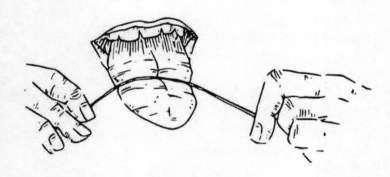

Licking Lures

For Zach, Rebecca, Boots, and The Mule

Just beyond the gill
I have to bite the liter to keep it
from blowing toward a tangle.
My tongue hides from the slime
on the line, a protective layer on the
trout we call grease pigs.

This *namegos* has risen like bread
or a cloud or that temper in a memory
unclasping swivels with gnawed cuticles
and nails. I brought hand to mouth
to blanket my blurting until my fingertips bled.
It never hurt till I had to pinch

> a stubborn blade
> from a folding knife
> or tangled laundry
> from washing machine drum

temper strikes loudly
when I remember my own quiet.
I have so many ripped jeans because
denim resists my jagged fingertip grip.

I learned to tie knots on a boat
that bobbed in the big lake,
rollers careened stern and bow.
Fishing line in wide wind demands patience,
it gusts a song about throbbing fingertips
and a hidden tongue, a blanket for words
stretched in my esophagus.

I get sea sick when I tie fishing line on dry land.
Reel clicks dilate my eardrums
as big as washing machines.
Why I'm tempted to lick the lure,
only the trout could say.

Salt Peanuts

Gillespie kissed
the brass like fists
his cheeks took blows gave style some pain.

He ground his teeth
to dust the crops
his tongue had sewn a quilt. He salts

his gums and lips,
collapsed his lungs,
his capillary flesh enticed

the maggot squirm.
I want my mouth to bloom
before I breathe or dizzy choke.

My nestled tongue
will horde a taste
against the palate painted spice.

The trumpet tastes
like farms at dawn
like swarms of bugs devoured gold.

Cranes Too Early, Trout Too Late

I won't wear mittens
after Spring Equinox.
Ziigwan chokes the ditches
with whips of red willow buds,
rockets really.
This cleaved salmon flesh sundown
has my dogs licking sandbag corpses
splayed on the riverbank.
More pines fell this year
than last. They lay supine
wriggle roots in the breeze.
Those arrowheads finally dropped life,
the ones hidden in the pith.

These dogs drag me like a janky skid over crusted snow
and I pretend we are going somewhere planned.
A gillnetter bundled tight chases fish holes, checks nets,
waves away *aandek*, *migizi*, and early *jiijaak*.
Their wings gust a chorus of caws at the net
full of gurgled yawps from black trout tongues.
This water song grinds into icy air:
                    grackle, caw, grunt, and krruu…
The beating winds shed scales.

Nectarine horizon makes me doubt this song,
laugh at snow drifts. They remind me
of waves I once knew.
The same wind shapes them, truly.

My knuckles are frozen
but the skin on my hands throbs
heated, gasping.
The dogs and I growl
trout death rattles
with every foot step that punches
through the gritty mantles.
We fall where the wind throws us.

Gnaw and Tame

I don't remove raw bones
from my front yard
so my dogs won't run far
when the wind blows
my front door open.

I don't know where
the bones come from.
My dogs carry them
dripping sinew and socket
but it's the marrow they want.

They gnaw and gnaw
at the core of mystery femurs
eyeing me to remember
that time eons ago
when they tamed my kind.

We bury dogs in the backyard
let them bring bones to the front.
We bury our bodies far off in the woods
where dogs dig holes, tame corpses.
Strong winds don't make them brittle.

Mètis Breakfast

Pipe tobacco rolled in bank receipts
smoked smooth from dirt to peat
with each sip of french pressed
and honeyed coffee. My body
is a bog. I wanted to quit
this winter. Two restless dogs
Banjo and Fiddle jig their feet
even in sleep. Rising Cloud sleeps shallow,
stirs hallow and aching for thunders.
The snow is trapezoid trapeze artists
dangled in funnels, swirling frost devils.
They tangle my drift driveway, the space between
our elk hide community drum *Waabishkaa Bizhiki Aanikwit*
and Sunday Mass at St. Kateri's Catholic Church.
Hyacinths are buried under a mantle of ice
and Fiddle nurses Banjo's busted duclaw
with his tongue, saliva pitch like a winter tuning fork.
If my body is a bog
I want bears to sleep in my arm pits
and flowers to bloom from my chest.
I swell with stifled earth.

Finger Painted and Blood Drawn

Goddammit the blood is back.

Measure life sustaining fluids
hoping fucking *hoping* mucus is slippery
enough for cells to live and bind
to be bound for life.

Doctor recommends a blood test.
Veins will tell the truth, right?
Spinning red vials separate hormones
the ones that luteinize
the ones that create universes
inside the female body to sustain life.
The intersection of arteries
is a divining rod.

Or intersecting legs
on intersecting bodies
slip taste buds behind ears
beyond creation
elated to begin again and again
and again and again.

We fuck to keep the blood away.
To remember a painting we want
to create someday with our child.

And we won't measure finger paintings
like blood in a bathroom sink.

Surefooted Spring-fed Salt Lick

Sheep and cattle and mink and rubber trees
were sheared and slaughtered to warm my feet.
But wool socks and stiff boots with hard soles betray me
on sheets of autumn ice, thin and desperate.
I am windswept, slick as bear grease.

Warblers gargle pinecone guts and bathe
in snowplow ruts. Sparks and salts wound
ditches but steadfast lavender stalks
shout against copper barberry brush.

Pine martens squint beyond the breeze,
that thorny tincture swept up in artesian spring.
Songs of wind-stripped seed heads drip and drain
one granule at a time. Whorled oils skate
full of grace on glare ice, that dance of winter balm.

Nuthatches flit necks in shrouds of naked lilac
then levitate bouncing on autumn gusts,
perchless frosted berry divers. My footfalls
must be salt licks when fangs are on the wind,
my hips set tense as bear traps.

There's a mountain lion in the brambles. She whispers
or purrs a melody thick with pursuit. Ears full of whiskers
somehow catch my scent, that flailing descent
hinged on my godforsaken midwestern *ope*,
that monosyllabic apology yelp.

Once plump and violet beach peas now leathered tatters
rattle a song about November's thump,
how surefooted tongues get severed
at the spring-fed salt lick, how frenzied paws
swindle callus treads out from under mink oiled boots.

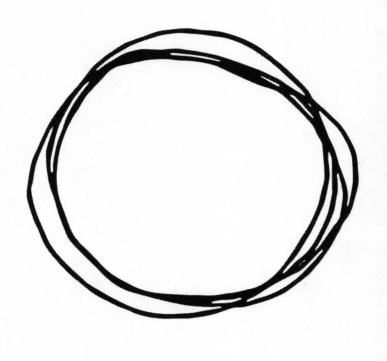

Section 2: Shout

"Luster Browne [...] meditated with shouts over panic holes, and he became a gardener by chance because flowers bloomed on the beds and meadows that heard his shouts."

- Gerald Vizenor, *Heirs of Columbus*

Daffodil Yawp

For Barb Kelly's Flourishes Crew

Every leaf is spirit
in retrospect. A flower can destroy
my frontal cortex. Wrecked spring
puddles in wretched rain drop
dew spots breathe hell toward
dawn. I'm melting. I'm melting.
Molting larva crept from mud,
the muffled insect crypt. Hallowed
gravel and hallelujah screams
grovel for snow banks to forgive
trash, needles, sand, and salt.
I've severed all but taproots.
Bacteriophage gnaw regardless
of salty soils from winter roads,
inflamed by sand scrapped
shovel scoops.
I'm only trying to compost myself,
to make the most
of myself, to choose
myself despite the piles of sweat
that stain my bed.
I'm yearning.

Dynamite Honey

Fought a lynx between my ears
woke up with blood in my mouth
brushed my teeth with razor blades
maple blossoms and hawk feathers

hand rubbed basil braided sweetgrass
grew four-leaf clovers between my toes
a million snowflakes fell the day I was born
lightning soldered winter bees beneath my crib

blue collar pollinators cauterized honey like dynamite
cranes stayed south that spring
I still pestle my head in honey comb mortar
a godawful bear thirsty for that deaf stream

where a cedar carcass floats to the biggest lake
ribbon waves curl lashes and entice
wink at my sober brain a promise of catharsis
to grow my hair longer than frogs can sleep

nectar and peat moss swell my tongue
that belly-up rosehip wintered over for the birds
I still hum to blue jays and chickadees
my suet lined throat hides a song with teeth

With Bloody Fangs Just Like Yours (*Wiindigo Mishkwiiwidoone*)

Rick Snyder fills his fish tank with Kalamazoo
and flosses his teeth with Flint.
He flicks a trickle in the hourglass
beneath his left wrist oxblood cufflink.
Neck tie Windsor knotted, breath tested to ignite
bluegills and Nestlé bubbles to remove their cysts.
Treasure chest piggy banks roll in muck,
eat shit, root in their own fecal earth
reconstructed. Rick dropped his wrist watch
switching sluices in a shuffle to deluge old lead.
He tells constituents to dive and drown
if they have to during the retrieval.
He lost track of time, let the shot-line slip
during descent when Enbridge flashed a Rolex.

Trickle some time
Down the line, won't ya?

Trickle time to the nine to fivers.
Trickle time to the college kids.
Trickle time to the hungry homeless.
Trickle time to the clever thieves.
Trickle time to the junkies.
Trickle time to the cold.
Trickle time to the bullied.
Trickle time to the bruised.
Trickle time to the suit-less.
Trickle time to the mothers and sisters.

Trickle time to the missing and murdered.
Trickle time to the job seekers,
       the stress and coffee tweakers.
Trickle time to the baristas.
Trickle time to the believers.
Trickle time to the can collectors,
       the bike stealers.
Trickle time to the meter maid.
Trickle time to the musicians who'll never make it.
Trickle time to the lawyers who swallow the barrel
       but never pull the trigger.
Trickle time to the tweeters, cheaters,
       the computer eaters.
Trickle time to those who hear the call
       of duty and join the ranks,
       get through boot camp to lose weight.
Trickle time to the water protectors, the scrapers
       the dilapidated soap-box actors.
Trickle time to the tight jean, thrift store cool kats
       who find themselves half a century back.
Trickle time to the tight lipped nurse.
Trickle time to the one in the hearse.
Trickle time to the vinyl record cigarette burns,
       barns that turn milk and honey to coins and paper.
Trickle time to the window breakers who dodge bullets
       and swerve Monte Carlos blasting Testament.
Trickle time to the muskrat divers and sandhill crane
       survivors.
Trickle time to the Lake Erie firefighters.
Trickle time to the pipe-lined straight
       between two great lakes.

Trickle time to the city with faith in locks that
 deteriorate.
Trickle time to the cold great lake that has no bottom,
 where dead bodies don't float.
Trickle time to the thunder talons that squeeze
 an old bad cat,
 the one you've abandoned us with,
 the one with bloody fangs just like yours.

Southpaw Gnome

Instead of gripping her thighs
I grabbed dishes and did em. Told myself
her crooked teeth were birds, if I made her smile
we'd escape from our prisons. Wings unclipped
and drowning in thunder since the third grade.
She felt like a hurricane.

But my soil baked hands rub the small of her back
and I sing her songs in the rain,
crack coffee beans between my teeth,
grit sand from beach bum shores.
Even *Gichi Gami* got oil leaks in her streams.

Not perfect just direct.
Converse to convert.
Electrify our hurtful claims.
When she taught me the recipe
the kitchen sink was soup stained.
I snapped a southpaw, rearranged the bleach
to where she could reach it.
Got cap full of clean left.

But colanders don't wash right and pasta ain't the dish
she like. We're broke and she wrote me a hundred notes.
Only one was a joke.

I forgot when we'd laugh how I'd grip her thigh,
we'd melt like wax, all because she really wants
a garden gnome.

Sweetgrass spoke to me between smoke and told me
tobacco got my lungs but it won't get my goat.
Touching skin can unfold wings and I'm scared
of the pretty things she tells me after the crocus rises.
Spring thunder cleans ozone early this year.

I'll cook her a hundred meals and only one
will be pasta. She'll laugh at spaghetti noodles
folded in sauce. Our garden will blossom
with flowers, not hastas. And I swear,
no matter the cost, there won't be wilt,
there will be want, she'll laugh,
I'll grip.

Pike

The hemlock seems to fly over the wharf and,
like cowardice, we forget that it sees everything.

From the fisherman's angular scars
to northern pike broken pin bones

cracked from thrashing in the flood of '72
when the water wolves saw-toothed needle bunches

disguised as underwater downy fledglings
but as soon as the water receded every pike

went belly-up. The bay was thick with whitefish
and sap ran quick that spring into summer.

There's a knotted rope of muscle above pike spines
that tastes like syrup, like the tip of a spear,

like thunderstruck hemlock groves. Spark encrusted
rhizomes tease needles to store piney poison.

Jawbone shapes story the fisherman's scars,
how he learned to spear from the trees,

to never fear a flood, and to grin like a pike.
He throws his head back and bares his molars,

belly guffaw all full of hazard and backbone,
flying with storied scars on his scaly skin.

Swamp Sap

I should run home before this tree falls, let winds drag me through conifers to a softer place.

Sap on my shoes. I climbed a pine again. In younger times I would get to the top and sway in the wind, breathe a distance over cattails to islands where wolves eat moose, old moonshine bottles sit where someone lived and died. Sloshed through muck and tall grasses with Blind Bob who adores deep books and Kentucky whisky. He is eighteen, without a job, and sleeps in baseball field dugouts where we bared orange slice grins in little league, laughed at fence jumpers and Crazy Dave who smuggled so many drugs into his brain his stories became something only us kids could laugh with. We weren't scared. Now we bust bottles and run from the city. Something is pushing us from the dugouts to run the islands not the bases. Alcohol sunsets burn guts and gums like rusty wrench sets and machine pitch swing an'a miss. Going, going, gone.

Someone should run for home before Blind Bob lets that bottle be his bat, his brain the ball.

Mouthwash

Joseph Half-G the Apache bends dirt roads
with his pickup, catches leaves between his teeth.
We call him that because
he can drink a half-gallon of whiskey in one night.
Enough for the whole tribe.
We call him that because
all Indians are plains Indians and he's Ojibwe.
Enough for the whole tribe.
At a hunting camp rave powered by generators
half the tribe watches him braid *wiingashk*
and hang it from a *wiigwas* cross beam
then around his neck. He fledges
like *migizi*. Half the tribe closes their eyes
and the other half is ghosts
that unbraid centuries of *miigwan*
before he hits the ground and sings
that old song of falling toward the sky.

Section 3: Eat

"Every time a page had been memorized, they could eat it."

-Leslie Marmon Silko, *Almanac of the Dead*

Cranberry Four-Ten

Grouse never flew past spruce trees
where I left medicines. But ruffled necks bent
vietnam vets in half when they chopped
and chopped, sprung from soggy ditches.

We always knew luxuries like chicken delicious.
Squirrel stew was finger lickin sacred,
unsweetened iron. Salt left holes in cheeks
and tongues felt beaten.

I set fire to the line where a white picket fence
retired its eggshell for cream after thirty years.
And screams from martens and fishers
couldn't bring back Ma's delicious dishes,
ones crispy and cooked in secret kitchens.

Grouse wings smear my memory
keeping my mouth shut to walk
past power lines and buckshot
road signs just to glimpse
where cranberries wintered
and the cleaving left Ma splintered
in pieces, crouched below
empty hummingbird sugar shacks.

The four-ten exploded
and missed the chop,
grazed cranberries,
now harvest never stops.

Casserole kisses rise in flames
that burnt divorce documents.
Thirty years of proof could've been photos
but were just recipes. I trust
Ma left the rest to me. Cayenne
cornbread and honey habanero. She told me
spice cuts wounds for sugars to pour in,
leaves the tongue swollen like drained swamps
make desperate frogs. She told me to kill all my birds
in cranberry bogs.

Moths and Hawks

What does the moth think of the hawk?

Do spiders despise the linemen
who weave nets of lightning
to trap songbirds?

Imitation can be fruitful in friendship
but fatal in a fight.

Like survival.

Like crabgrass claws shucking corn cobs,
there's a moth that nibbles eyelids off sleeping hawks.

Imagine having extraordinary vision
and the inability to blink.

Imagine a white bear rolled in mud
for camouflage soaked in rain
replaced snow, a warmed north.

Every advantage washes off.

There's a reason hawks don't harvest
from the water. Moth chrysalides don't sink
and revenge would be too sweet.

Spuds Are Heavy

Sunflowers so tall I could stand
atop my Pa's shoulders and barely
peer over the yellow-petal landscape.

Pa said *dirt's what's under your fingernails.*
Everything else is soil. We grew tomato, zucchini,
corn, peppers, squash, and cucumbers but never potatoes.

Our yard was a wide open splayed book.
I was sent to pick weeds, had to fill three bushels
to leave the garden. I grew up a sunflower child.

Death metal and leather-jacket
Wings burst from chrysalis, northern migration
mimicry. In the pale winter flicker of local IGA,

Pa picked up a ten-pound sack of potatoes
chucked it into the squeaky-wheeled cart.
Pa said *potatoes grow anywhere.*

Pa taught me secret yields in cabbage, too.
We never grew potatoes, but we ate them
whenever the garden harvest depleted.

He never met his Irish-lawyer birth father.
Every phone call gets hung up.
Not sure which end commits to the ending.

Pa knows his father is Irish and a lawyer.

Never trust lawyers,
embrace my heritage.

I don't know how Pa chose which trait
to value, which to hate, but it must've been
something in the soil.

A ghost of a potato sack counter-weighs my noose.
Ramen noodles might be the new cabbage
but I've always flipped couches for change,

cashed in trash-found beer cans,
and sang the blues for potato money.
That noose rope never slips when I'm broke.

The spuds are heavy even as memories.
When I ate my first raw potato Pa said *you'll get worms,*
but I didn't. My dog had worms then.

All puppies are born with worms.
He was a fluffy little black and white
floppy-eared pup that defecated

brown squirming shit for a week. All I had
in my poor pantry was Ramen Noodles, beef flavor,
the kind that turn brown and slither off the fork.

The stove broke so I microwaved those noodles
choked 'em down. Next day my stomach refused
slimy noodles. Behind the Ramen packs was an old potato.

I remembered *they can grow anywhere*. I told Pa about eating
my first raw potato and about my pup's wormy stool.
Pa is Irish and Potawatomi, has a head like a potato.

His face ripened with laughter and the two of us cried.
That year was the first year my dad grew potatoes
in the garden. He gave me one and told me

grow it somewhere, anywhere.

The Doors Left Unlocked

Kids around the drum offer *aseema*
earthy tobacco of reciprocity
for their grandpa.

Miigwech minobimaadezewin
nadamoshin nagamowin, idiwag.

Their hands press like pipestones
through the drum skin
elk hide pliable
as a candied fruit sheet.

Ozaywazibi giizis ombigwashkaawni
nooskwaanzo gidiskse ogondashkway
bashkijii miskwii widaamikane ziigwaan.
Bakade minokiwan.

Young crane says
spirits dance if
you sing long enough
the doors unlock.

Minokiwan wiisini
oshki-nagamowin.

I don't know what kids pray for
but there's never *aseema*
on the floor
when we put the drum away.

Juncos and Buntings

Look at the rainbow
in the fog
above the barn
where the pigeons
throw themselves
into the hayloft.
          You can see it
at this angle
from before you told me
how hard it was the day
my car broke down.
I slept in town that night
          miles away
from you and your womb
both only warmed by the bog
and our two snoozing dogs.
Don't hold your breath
but this is what it sounds like
          before I cry.
Mourning doves coo hard
like fresh sheared lambswool
and this sharp horizon lacerates
queen anne's lace in the ditch
but the Mountain Ash in the field
have berries that
          just hang in there
happy to feed every single
nuthatch and chickadee,
even the juncos and buntings

that visit for the snows.

You can see it
miles away
before I cry.
        Just hang in there.

What the Soil Forgot

Take a big red cloth, fill that sucker with tobacco
pray while the red melon of medicine
smolders wet with juices and soggy smoke
as soon as the first thunders arrive.
I've learned to forget these instructions all winter long
but I do pray to wildfires and frozen lakes.

Ode'miin are the first to fruit.
I've seen red vines burst in frost.
Pa was there when I feasted my name,
said that his sled dog mom was there in spirit.
He knows I'm teaching him what he forgot.
Imagine all the berries I've buried
under winters of my tightly folded arms.
Pa sees red in the snow and the anger,
calls it blood memory.

I know a woman who carries ziplock bags of banana peels
in her purse and plants them under every rose bush
that doesn't blush enough when she walks by.
Also, the ones with too many thorns—
there can only be so many barbs
in a garden. She's magic with the soil.
She knows about root conversations.

A young man asked me why there's so much poison ivy
at the edge of the swamp. I told him it's Labrador tea
     mashkigaabo.
He gathered a handful in a bag and I told him to ask bears

help him boil the medicine. I feared for the fuzzy orange
      underside
of that leaf when it danced under his gaze. We gnawed
      wintergreen
in early spring and nod at the brambles and burs on our
      legs.

I can forget how to breathe when she looks at me.
We have that effect on each other.
Same way a low berry bends to the ground
and forgets to feed anything but itself.
There's a circle to it, like seeds covered in soil
sowed with soil sowed seeds. That's the cycle.
That's love. It doesn't need us.
We are just here to breathe
before the petals rot
and taste what the soil forgot.

Quill Remembers the Oxbow

Stand in the pollen
of a tamarack thicket you'll see what I mean
by Delirium dance. Golden conifer clumps
pepper this swamp. Reeds and fungus
thick with life, microbial heat can melt the ice.

You are the reason
I return there. Not believing till I bathe
in that mud to return the blood
of primordial gunk. I promise you,
no amount of asphalt or glass can redeem
the junk you keep behind the bathroom cupboard
where even the flies won't dance.

Us dogs cower
from your collection, your bottles
of pills, enhancers, shots,
and plastic necromancers.
Come with me and gather the goop.
Cattails snarl erect on reeds; islands form a sacred hoop.
Oxbow bent backwards—not prescription or vision,
no healing incision. Stand with me now
in the pollen of tamaracks.
Rip the cattail up from root.
Feast with me on primordial shoots.

This is where us dogs play, flies dance,
toads sing, and cranes romance.

This is the place I was telling you.
You were raised where pine needles drop
and water won't freeze.

Caution like Fiver

She saw the jumping water
filled with blood at sunset,
our own little watership down,
gill nets and sugar buckets.

I spoke to pregnant stomachs,
whispered to the unborn,
felt for the kick.

Lit candles, said prayers,
chained knuckles for smooth séance,
third-eye in the candle wick.

Whisky poured down
the clogged drain. She sang
all day, prayed for rain to end.

When it hit, my arms
twitched. Hair pulled
by some big sphere.

I don't know if it would be
or had been, but it stretched
my arms and eyes for miles,

shook rabbits from behind
my ears. It felt like a flea detained,
like Fiver gagging on cowslips.

Section 4: Tell

"Honeybee, / go and tell the starling / to go and tell my darling / to hurry home to me."

-Connie Converse, "Honeybee"

Cleaning Trout

Young man with a switchblade pen can't decide
if he will fight or write about loss.

Young woman with clay molded false nails
a blue-gray she says is sparkled
stole classroom glitter and pressed
her fresh-did nails toward the bottle bottom.
Her reach was to repair mens' stares
from side-eye trout
back to gentle bears.
She watched benevolent gardeners plant seeds
whisper *grow grow please grow*
season into combines and thrashers
to harvest spoils. She won't be
the grain truck
or the good luck
but the *get fucked*
her ma screamed at the match
that lit her pa's clothes.
She wept lighter fluid.

Youngman's father rips lids off
tallboys of Beast with his teeth
and drinks like a fish.
After clanging can after can
his butterfly knife mouth rusts shut
a cocoon of tiger swallowtails and fruit bats
claw his rippled mouth's roof.
He never sleeps dry

or without sweating, suppressing.

He remembers young women with false nails
who stole knives to clean trout.

Honey High and Nectar Prone

My amygdala is broken.
I'm drowning in my own prop-wash.
Hollyhocks won't climb the lattice
because I've planted them in sand instead of soil.
It has nothing to do with the vine ties
or even the sunshine.

Gimme some sugar to season the depression.
No, dandelion wine doesn't prove there's a heaven.

Swallow nutmeg if you want to lose your mind.
Or remember that time you helped
bong-blitzed salvia stunner wipe his saliva.
Or the times you drove him to the baker to buy
pounds of poppy seeds, lied about bake sales
and fundraising. The blue dots buzzed
a song he loved in the coffee maker.
You could see the seeds between his teeth when he grinned
and grinned as he placed forget-me-nots
one stem at a time into crushed can
filter holes crusted with resin
and called it a bouquet.

Sipping cold medicine can wilt flowers.
Nasturtium petals are peppered flesh.

Why do we season what we can't eat
and medicate what we can't treat?

If I was a bumble-bee
I'd go extinct, too.

She's Got Sugar

Rot gut and a split tongue.
Hanging out with addicts
can do that to ya, she says.
She says *bitch* a lot
when she's with childhood friends.
She built a yellow kitchen
with yellow lights
but won't drink yarrow tea
or watch paper cranes mellow
in narrow sunlight.
Her singing can shake the silverware
but won't ever wake the baby.
She never wraps the vacuum chord
but brushes her teeth twice a day.
She'll offer amends
but can't catch a break.
Her clean laundry wrinkles bundled in baskets
but her lashes curl like iris petals
placed on caskets. She tells me her dreams
are shorelines that disobey the moon.
She hides forty-gallon trash bags
folded tissue size and calls them
Shunk Road suitcases,
the rez road that bears the name
of her crooked teeth.

Churn

Her churning toes polished black
like a mole nose blindly burrowed into his thigh,
a sign language on skin like Helen Keller.
She told him for sure that
he's falling down relativity.
He misses staircases and doorways.
It was flint to steel to the bone.

Hemlock Ain't For Hillbillies

For Gramma "Poof" Sgriccia

Hummingbird silhouettes
eyelash tongue flits blood red sugar water
brings me back to Gramma's on the bay.

Bubbles, frogs, creeks that dry,
sand dunes, pine cones,
and whip-weed shin bones.
She was born in a boxcar
but we aren't strong enough
for the Hemlock Society.
Gravesites aren't bound by priests
but by elders who carry stories
like Grandma Poof's dream walk
into Lake Michigan—it refuses to stop.

Tomato Juice

Mom speaks to spirits
better than the priest,
drinks beer with tomato juice
in the Upper Peninsula.
I don't know
how she laughs and trembles
at funerals. Grandma Poof
taught the art of thriftiness—
extract the worthless, make it shine.

Grandma Poof taught Mom
about sand dunes and Petoskey stones
and beach glass. Mom hovers over the beach
carefully like Vesuvius over Pompeii.
Sand seems to melt under her gaze.
She wants her beach glass urn
flown over Lake Superior and dropped.
The gales sting my skin,
fold waves like a million mouths
laughing and gargling stones to sand.

You Must Be a Murder

For O.C.S. kids

Just one crow caw won't keep the wolves at bay.
Noodin winds could not (re)move empty hot cheeto bags
frozen in parking lot puddle ruts. Obsidian beak taps
broke framed glass. School bus with windows shot out
could be a feast or a carcass.

You must be a murder to keep the wolves at bay.
Trailers stitched together grin and moan a circus
accordion teather. Sap spills into elder buckets,
minaadendimowin. Taste the teachings as flowers
taste the bats. Mourn the silvernose,
cheeto diabetes,
alcohol absentees,
abusive aggressors.
Forgive disease with cedar sweats.
Medicines are seeds you must plant.

You must be a murder to mourn the wolves away.
Remember Nanabozho farts and cries after every smirk
and trick. The rez ain't just a map dot but a revolving door
of memory to when mukwa had tails
and every time uncles go to jail
and thunder was birds
and when one   in   three   Indigenous   girls
won't speak until someone asks
                    tell me, please, remember.
Remember.

You must remember a murder of crows is spirits at play.
Wolves follow sun flares shook off *aandek miikwan*,
feathers slice arrows toward meat. Aim in one direction
point another. Let the wolves chase.
Know their breath, teach them to call for you
during hungry moons, howling.
Patch bus window bullet holes
with empty hot cheeto bags
and feast on teachings that always ask us
          tell me, please.
Remember.

Thousands of Frogs Croaking Purple

The blues aren't really blue they're purple.
Above sunsets over tamarack and pine
shingwaak meditate and shelter drunks.
But all I hear are thousands of frogs croaking purple.

That grandmother whitepine negotiates
for the State and Rez cops.
She must have sheltered so many mosquitos
and parties. She's a legend on this rez.
Tamaracks rebloom every year
but this grandmother holds her needles,
the ones buried between roots.
Glass shards scrawl stories
between rhizome and earth.

Nokomis shingwauk exonerates the man
with an otter mustache. She practices acquittal
as he rests beneath her everyday on his *bimose*
sojourn between the rat trap where he gets loaded
and the edge of the rez where he loads up.
He curls 24 ouncers.
The trail elbow eyes his conviction,
prolongs his trial. His leathered brown skin
like an abandoned briefcase.

They call him purple, bent toward the setting sun,
like *Original Indigenous*. He suppresses
and we remember a sacred number of things:
       Veteran. Rapist. Drunk. Dementia.

That pine can only support his burden for so long
before his branch is abandoned. He is too stubborn
or repressed to see the tamaracks budding each spring.

I want to purse my lips
and point his attention to deciduous needles
but I just can't.
All I can hear are thousands of frogs croaking purple.
And pine roots barking dementia.

Nibi Bimaadezewin (A Prayer for Travel)

Gichigami n'donkoskiche
minawah zibi manidoo.

Mashkiig nadamoshin
bimaadezewin.

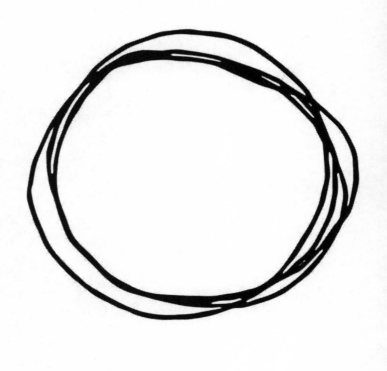

About the Author

Tyler Dettloff is an Anishinaabe Métis, Italian, and Irish writer, professor, musician, gardener, and water protector raised on the edge of the Delirium Wilderness. He currently lives in Gnoozhekaaning (Bay Mills, Michigan) and teaches College Composition at Lake Superior State University. He has earned a B.S. in English and a dual track M.A. in Literature and Pedagogy from Northern Michigan University. Mostly, he enjoys walking along rivers with his wife Daraka and daughter Meadow Minokami and through swamps his dogs Banjo and Fiddle.

About the Artist

Claire Moore - heART in hand DESIGN

*he*ART *in hand* DESIGN is a moniker implying Claire holds her heart, or passion, in her hand...the very hand that clicks, paints, draws, and brings that third cup of coffee to her lips as she creates. She loves what she does: a concept apparent in the breadth of her work.

A Northern Michigan University alum with a Bachelor's in Graphic Communication and Marketing, Claire served on the Marquette Arts & Culture Advisory Committee for several years before helping form the Marquette Artist Collective and their gallery space in Michigan's beautiful Upper Peninsula. She is an exhibiting artist, freelance designer, and an arts and craft facilitator at several local non-profits. Claire will be pursuing her Master's of Fine Arts this fall.

Find her designs and artwork at www.heartinhand.design or follow her progress on Instagram at @heartinhanddesign.

Acknowledgements

I would like to extend my gratitude to the following publishers for supporting my poems through publication: *Heartwood Literary Magazine* for publishing "Daffodil Yawp" in Issue 5; *River Heron Review* for publishing "Metis Breakfast" in Issue 2.1; *Santa Ana River Review* for also publishing "Metis Breakfast" in Fall/Winter 2019 Issue; *Cutthroat, a Journal of the Arts* for publishing "Juncos and Buntings," "Cleaning Trout," and "To Keep Away Crows Feet" in Issue 24 vol. 1 & 2; *Jelly Bucket* for publishing "Thousands of Frogs Croaking Purple," "Cranes Too Early, Trout Too Late," "Mouthwash," "Dynamite Honey," "Surefooted Spring-fed Salt Lick," and for featuring an Anishinaabemowin glossary and interview in Issue 9; *Third Coast* for publishing "Pike" in Issue 48; *Swimming with Elephants Publications* for publishing "To Keep Away Crows Feet" in their weekly writes series August 2019 and for publishing my first chapbook collection; and *SwEP* guest contest judges Maxine Peseke and Gina Marselle for choosing "Belly-up Rosehip" as a contest winner and writing such wonderfully encouraging reviews.

These poems would not be where they are in their truest forms without the constructive criticism and feedback from my friends and readers. I met each of them at Northern Michigan University while working on my M.A. degree and am so glad to have them in my life. My heartfelt thanks to Tim Johnston for perspective on art and voice; Sarah Bates for encouragement and help with ending poems; Ashley Goedker for strengthened images and emboldened actions; and Dr. Amy Hamilton for guidance and challenges.

I'm very thankful my family encourages my creative work. A *chi-miigwech* to Mom for support, wine laughs, and strength; Bob Quinn for clowning, wordplay, and teaching me to throw a proper tarp; *Gnoozhekaaning* for youthful laughter and lessons around *Waabishka Bizhiki Aanikwit*; Dad for belly laughs, wonder, and understanding dogs; Banjo and Fiddle for curiosity and security; Ryan for humor and dynamics; Atticus and Phoenix for imagination and fears overcome; Song birds for looking me in the eye and singing all around me; Bears for sleeping all winter long and scrounging the best; Cedar for grace and abundance; Water for being clean and quenching; Spring equinox full moon and Thunderers for bringing me my beautiful, perfect daughter; Meadow Minokami for smiling with her eyes and choosing me as a father, *giizaagin n'daanis*; and Daraka for listening to my stubborn repetition and knowing these poems and songs are *debwewin*, true.

And thank you, reader, for supporting my collection of poetry. I hope you find everything from catharsis to joy to pain and delirium in these pages.

Miigwech,

Tyler Dettloff
Ozawa Binese

Also available from
Swimming with Elephants Publications, LLC

Thalassophile
Abigayle Goldstein

the fall of a sparrow
Katrina K Guarascio

Shorn: apologies and vows
Benjamin Bormann

I've Been Cancelling Appointments with My Psychiatrist for Two Years Now
Sean William Dever

They Are All Me
Christina Dominque

Unease at Rest
Wil Gibson

bliss in die/ unbinging the underglow
Bassam

from below/ denied the light
Paulie Lipman

Language of Crossing
Liza Wolff-Francis

Find More Publications at:
swimmingwithelephants.com

Swimming with Elephants
P U B L I C A T I O N S

Made in the
USA
Lexington, KY